Piano Literature

BO 1

An Introduction Through Folk Songs and Singing Games

Arrangements by David Kraehenbuehl

Selected and Correlated by Frances Clark

Edited by Louise Goss

Cover Design: Debbie Johns

© 1964 Summy-Birchard Music
division of Summy-Birchard, Inc.
Exclusive print rights administered by
Alfred Music Publishing Co., Inc.
All Rights Reserved.   Printed in USA.

ISBN-10: 0-87487-125-5
ISBN-13: 978-0-87487-125-8

Preface

In designing the series, PIANO LITERATURE OF THE 17TH, 18TH AND 19TH CENTURIES, we found that there were almost no original keyboard works by master composers easy enough for Level 1 students. Thus the problem for Book 1 of the series was to find a suitable substitute as preparation for the volumes that follow.

What more natural introduction to great piano literature itself than another part of our musical heritage—folk songs and singing games in simple, tasteful piano arrangements?

The 1964 revised edition includes favorite folk songs from many countries, arranged for piano by David Kraehenbuehl, composer-in-residence at the New School for Music Study in Princeton.

We believe that these folk songs for young pianists serve as ideal preparation, both technically and musically, for the rich heritage of real piano literature that follows in subsequent volumes.

Frances Clark

Contents

London Bridge
Is Washed Away

London Bridge is washed away!
Dance on, my ladies all!
London Bridge is washed away!
Sing high, gain-de-day!

AMERICAN

Let ev'ry good fellow now join in the song,
Vive la compagnie!
Success to each other and pass it along,
Vive la compagnie!

Vive la Compagnie!

FRENCH

5

Old MacDonald Had a Farm

Old MacDonald had a farm, E-I-E-I-O!
And on that farm he had a duck, E-I-E-I-O!
With a quack, quack here, and a quack, quack there,
Here a quack, there a quack, ev'rywhere a quack, quack,
Old MacDonald had a farm, E-I-E-I-O!

AMERICAN

Three blind mice! Three blind mice!
See how they run! See how they run!
They all ran after the farmer's wife,
Who cut off their tails with a carving knife.
Did you ever see such a sight in your life
As three blind mice!

Three Blind Mice

TRADITIONAL

7

Home on the Range

Oh, give me a home where the buffalo roam,
Where the deer and the antelope play,
Where seldom is heard a discouraging word,
And the skies are not cloudy all day.

Expressively

AMERICAN

8

Sleep, baby, sleep,
Thy father guards the sheep;
Thy mother shakes the dreamland tree,
And down come all the dreams on thee;
Sleep, baby, sleep.

Sleep, Baby, Sleep

GERMAN

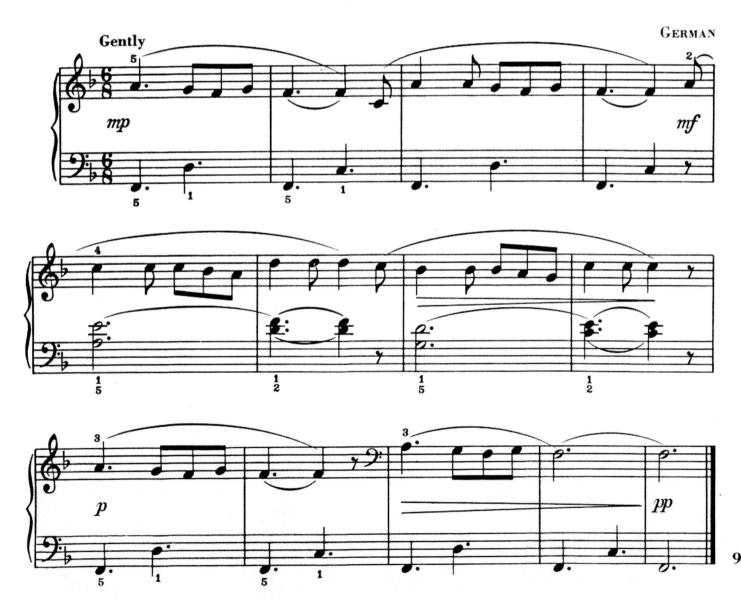

9

Ach, du lieber Augustin!

(Duet)

Oh, you poor dear Augustin,
Augustin, Augustin,
Oh, you poor dear Augustin,
Everything's gone!

Money's gone, sweetheart's gone,
All is gone, all is gone,
Oh, you poor dear Augustin,
Everything's gone!

GERMAN

With vigor

10

11

Pop! Goes the Weasel

All around the cobbler's bench,
The monkey chased the weasel,
The weasel thought 'twas all in fun,
Pop! goes the weasel.

AMERICAN

Lively

12

Drink to me only with thine eyes,
And I will pledge with mine;
Or leave a kiss within the cup,
And I'll not ask for wine.

Drink to Me Only
with Thine Eyes

Very smoothly

ENGLISH

13

Hot Cross Buns

Hot cross buns!
Hot cross buns!
One-a-penny, two-a-penny,
Hot cross buns!

ENGLISH

Vigorously

14

On top of Old Smoky,
All cover'd with snow,
I lost my true lover,
A-courtin' too slow.

On Top of Old Smoky

AMERICAN

15

Juanita

(Duet)

Soft o'er the fountain,
Ling'ring falls the southern moon;
Far o'er the mountain,
Breaks the day too soon.

Expressively

SPANISH

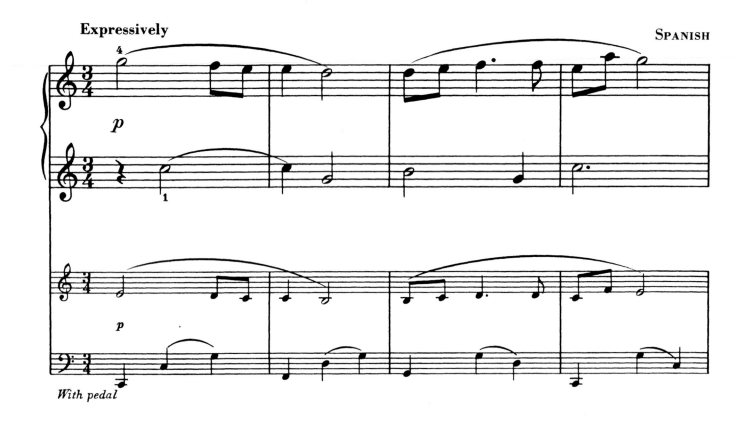

With pedal

16

mf very expressively

mf

17

Where, oh where is pretty little Susie?
Where, oh where is pretty little Susie?
Where, oh where is pretty little Susie?
Way down yonder in the pawpaw patch.

Pawpaw Patch

AMERICAN

19

A-Hunting We Will Go!

ENGLISH

Lively

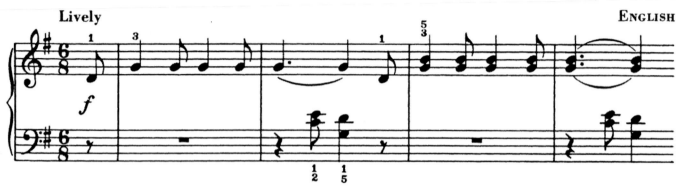

20

As I was going up London Hill,
London Hill, London Hill,
As I was going up London Hill,
One cold, frosty morn.

London Hill

ENGLISH

21

Clapping Song

MEXICAN

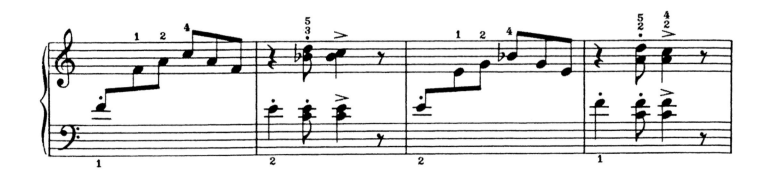

As the blackbird in the spring,
'Neath the willow tree,
Sat and piped, I heard him sing,
Sing of Aura Lee.

Aura Lee

AMERICAN

23

Can You Play This, My Friend?

Can you play this, my friend, my friend?
Can you play this, my friend, my friend?
Can you play this on your tiny flute?
Can you play this on your broken lute?

CANADIAN

Jauntily

Sleep, my child, and peace attend thee,
All through the night.
Guardian angels God will send thee,
All through the night.

All Through the Night

WELSH

25

The Jolly Miller

(Duet)

There was a jolly miller once,
Who lived by the River Dee,
He worked and sang from morn till night,
No lark more blithe than he.

And this the burden of his song,
Forever used to be:
"I care for nobody, no not I,
And nobody cares for me!"

Boldly

ENGLISH

26

To Market

ENGLISH

Now 'neath the silver moon, ocean is glowing,
O'er the calm billows, soft winds are blowing,
   Who now will sail with me,
    Sail with me, o'er the sea?
Santa Lucia, Santa Lucia.

Santa Lucia

ITALIAN

The British Grenadiers

(Duet)

Some talk of Alexander, and some of Hercules,
Of Hector and Lysander, and such great names as these;
But of all the world's brave heroes
There's none that can compare,
With a tow, row, row, row, row, row,
The British Grenadiers!

In march time

ENGLISH

31

Minka

Minka's eyes are sad and teary,
She must work although she's weary.
Life, it seems, is rather dreary,
Life is sad for Minka.

RUSSIAN

32